Author's Note

Memories of being with those we love
are precious little gifts from our lives.
They nest in our brains and later rise
above everything else residing there,
determined to survive.

It's hard to imagine those memories
leaving because they are with us
for so long. They comfort us

Visit my website at:
http://www.makingmagicstudio.com/

This book is dedicated to all the Mamas and Grandma everywhere. May your heart be lifted and your soul be blessed.

A Mother's Heart

A mother's hear functions
in such a wonderful way.
It holds all the love to fill all
of her little one's needs.
The love remains constant day after day,
happy serving others and
performing good deeds.

God alone truly understands a mother's heart
because he designed it and planted love there.
No one else can play a mama's part
or dispense such understand care.

Mothers know what is best
every day for each child
and God renews their special kind of love.
The most stubborn child can be beguiled
by mother's special wisdom from above.

Mommy

Mommy fixes all my boo-boos
with her gentle caring hands.
She gets me dressed and ties my shoes
and fixes broken toys with glue
and rubber bands.

Mommy makes breakfast, lunch and dinner
and helps me eat it with my spoon too.
Mommy helps me play and be a winner.
Without Mommy, what would I do?

Mommy reads me a good story book
and teaches me to say prayers and sing.
I love the way my Mommy's eyes look
when I learn to do a new thing.

Through Mama's Eyes

I always wondered why Mama saw things
as much better than most other people see them.
Mama saw snowflakes and bunnies and
dragonfly wings,
where others saw cold pesky animals and
buzzing, biting bug things.

Mama saw grass greener and clouds as
wonderful soft pillows on a breeze.
Others hated grass that had to be cut, and
saw clouds bringing too much rain.
Mama saw snow as a wonderful reason
to feed birds under Winter trees.
Others thought it was a nuisance that gave
them grief and pain.

I think it was Mama's faith in God
that helped her see a different way.
I always remember the positive things
and how she described them to me.
Thank you God for letting me see like Mama did
every bright new day.
He me please to teach my little ones to see like
Mama and me.

Mommie's Helper

Mommy says God is here to help her each day,
but she needs me to be a helper for her too.
Sometimes I don't really know a good way
to help with big jobs my Mommy
has to do.

I will just try to do the little things she tells me to
like pick up my toys and eat all my lunch,
share with baby sister and find
her little lost shoe.
I bet these will help Mommy a whole bunch.

I really love my Mommy so every much
and she loves me and little Sissy too.
Without our Mommy's loving touch
we wouldn't know what to do.

Mommy Is Always Here

Sometimes when I have a really bad dream
and wake up scared and crying in my bed
and just have to let out a real loud scream
'cause I am sure something is under my bed.

Mommy comes quickly and scoops
me up with a sweet smile,
holds me tightly and says there's nothing
to fear.

She whispers softly in my ear and
rocks me for a while.
I'm so glad Mommy is always here!

Mother's Quiet Acceptance

When Mother's heart is breaking
her children will never know.
Mother's worries are always unspoken
and all the while her smile still glows.

Mothers guard their little ones happiness
no matter the cost to themselves.
Only God hears about her helplessness
as she relies on His merciful goodness.

God supplies the strength that mothers need
to do the job He gave them.
He supplies the love they all use to feed
to the children given to them by Him.

Mothers accept things as they are
not how they wish it might be
They know God's leading them afar
and trust that He always will be.

Mother's Places

It makes no difference where mothers come from
Their hearts are the same in different places.
They all love their children when they come
no matter their homelands or races.

They all are willing to sacrifice, to give
their children the best upbringing they
can possible achieve.
Mothers everywhere usually don't rest
until all the childrens needs they receive.

A mother's love is an awesome thing
in a home she maintains for her little ones.
She tries to make each child's heart sing.
She understands every heart inside
her daughters and sons.

A Mother's Nights

Mothers are so busy during the day
it's hard to find time to write or sketch.
Talented mommies have to find a way
to create while families yawn and stretch.

This might leave them tired the next day
but they smile and keep right on going.
They know talents not used fade away
so they use their gifts while the kids
are growing.

They know that it will be worth whatever
the cost to use those gifts God
has give them.
They know their talents won't be lost
so they dedicate all their creations to Him.

Mother's Memories

When mothers grow old and meek and mild
their minds wander a bit
but they recall all about each child
and her stories always seems to fit.

Whichever child's story she is recalling
is etched deep within her heart.
Whether they played nicely or were
always brawling
each one in her memory owns a
special part of mama's heart.

Mothers worry about their children even
when they are old and God still
hears that Mother's prayer for her child.
Prayer can accomplish miracles I'm told
when it comes from an aged Mother
for her lost child.

My Mommy Loves Art

My Mommy likes to create nice works of art
I like to do that sitting right beside her
I always try to add my marks and do my part
to make Mommy's art work look lots better.

Mommy wants me to use my own paper
but I like hers a whole bunch more better.
Mommy hands me clay and a little shape
but I want to draw a letter right in the
middle of her paper.

Mommy and me don't see eye to eye
about her art
but she still loves little me anyway
I guess mommies just have a big heart
and do art when kids nap every day.

After School

Sometimes when things at school cause dismay
I know when Mama and I get back tonight
everything will start to seem better, even okay.
After Mama and I have talked things
are usually alright.

Mama has a way of seeing things
in a broader way than me.
She thinks of possibilities and reasons
a different way, seeing things
that don't even occur to me.
She always can figure out how to save the day.

I hope that I can be that smart
when I have kids of my own.
I know Mama will sure do her part
to help me get smarter by the time
I'm grown.

My Mommy's So Smart

When I ask Mommy a question about anything
she gives me the best answer right away
I know Mommy's answers will bring
knowledge for me to win every day.

I asked her how she got so smart about everything
Mommy told me she studied really hard
She said learning makes her heart just sing
and teaching me makes her feel the very
same way.

Mommy says learning about the Bible
is important
because it teaches us about God's love
It shows us how we can do things that
we think we can't
while God's love guides learning from up above.

Mama's Love

Most human love lasts only a little while
often shallow and only skin deep.
The warmth of a mother's loving smile
is forever something we can keep.

Mama is always there for her children
even after they are grown up and gone.
Mama's loving heart is still there even when
we think we're abandoned and all alone.

Only God could sustain such unselfish love
so Mama keeps Him close within her heart.
It's this guidance coming to her from above
that gives Mama's steadfast love to impart.

Mama's Flowers

Mama's flower garden looked so pretty and light
and smelled so delightfully sweet
I can still remember the colors, pastels
so vividly bright and all of the
butterflies coming to her garden to meet.

Early Sunday mornings Mama picked
flowers for the church's alter
She would always sing softly over
her colors and greenery
to carefully arrange in a bouquet for God's alter.
Mama's flowers matched Heaven's
own scenery.

I know God was pleased, because only the
best blossoms would do.
Mama wanted to honor Him with
the best that she had.
And taught us that we should too.
Remembering Mama's church bouquets
makes my heart feel glad.

Mama's Quiet Time

Mama didn't get much quiet time
when all of us were small.
Somehow though she managed to
find a few minutes each day
to stop and sit down and
summon us with her sweet call
Then she would start to read from her Bible
and bow her head to pray.

All of us looked forward to this special
time each day
when we could spend quiet time with
our dear mother
It was a joy to hear my mama read her Bible
and pray.
Now all grown up I cherish my mother
above any other.

Mama knew faith was the most
important thing
that she could ever leave to her children
She taught us to read and pray
about everything
God let her see it in all of us
before he life came to an end.

Mama's Rocking Chair

I remember Mama's rocking chair
and how I loved to be rocking in her arms
Sometimes I wish I could go back there
and hear her singing about little animals
on farms.

Sometimes mama sang about the blue birds
or a kitty cat.
The best sons Mama sang told about Jesus
loving little me.
There is no better memory than that.
Mama rocking and sweetly singing
a song to me.

When I have a little one of my own
I will have a rocking chair
I'll place it where we can be alone
I'll rock and sing and Mama's love
will always surround us there.

When Mothers Become Grandmothers

When mothers become grandmothers
it's really lots more fun for them.
They have more time than when they
were mothers
to love grandchildren and just
play with them.

If they get tired the kids can go back
to their house
and grandmothers can take a long nap.
Grandmothers keep homes
quiet as a mouse.
Mommies take noise all over the map.

Don't worry Mommy your day will come.
You will be a grandma someday too.
Then you'll be the one with a quiet home
where you can have a nap too.

Time Standing Still

When mothers think of their children
their whole world seems to just stand still
They remember all of the moments
when their eyes with happy
tears would fill.

When mothers' children accomplished
a special thing,
their proud hearts would skip a beat and swell.
Then those mothers' happy hearts
would surely sing.
Of course then all their friends
they just had to tell.

Children never lose their special place
within their mother's loving heart.
God planted that seen in the heart's
innermost space.
From that God given place
it will never depart.

For Mama Grose

Now she plantin' flowers in Heaven above
beneath a sheltering angel's wing
She's bathed in the light of purest love
Listening to a Heavenly chorus sing.

Pink roses in front of a pearl covered gate
pansies by the streets of gold
Daffodils to blossom early and
geraniums for blooming late.
Pastels pale mixed with colors bold.

Smiling down, Mama says:
"Don't feel sad, wipe away every tear.
Think of me when plants bloom
in the very early Spring.
By the time you all join me here
There will be flowers around everything.

Stitches

A special coat with a pieced raccoon collar,
a pretty pink suit with bunny fur buttons,
an embroidered skirt and ball fringe curtains,
a black cape for a monster beauty contest,
a gray wren costume for an
important school play,
Mama always tried to stitch these things
in a day.

Letters and numbers on a Little League shirt,
hand puppets enough for a whole school class,
a top to match a baby doll skirt,
wedding dresses and bridesmaid gowns,
baby clothes crocheted and sewn,
little stuffed people with smiles and frowns,
lots of play outfits with hats and crowns.

Over the years the scrap creations have grown.
The things are gone but memories
sewn in remain,
of us on Mama's lap when most of the
things were sewn.

Will You

Will you be there for me
when I have grown old?
Your strong hand will I see
for my weak one to hold?

If I could I'd spare you
any having to care for me.
I promise to keep trying to do
all that God allows me to see.

I'd like to choose to go back now
to be with then angles again
Only God really knows how
to see us through the pain.

www.ingramcontent.com/pod-product-compliance
Lightning Source LLC
Chambersburg PA
CBHW042339150426
43195CB00001B/43